How to Speak

Fluent
Lovey-Dovey

in 11 languages
in 24 hours

written/illustrated
packaged/spoken by
Karen Salmansohn

♥ universe
Publishing ♥

Serious non-lovey-dovey legalese

First published in the United States of America in 2002 by UNIVERSE PUBLISHING A Division of Rizzoli International Publications, Inc. 300 Park Avenue South New York, NY 10010 ✿ Copyright © 2002 by Karen Salmansohn ✪ All rights reserved. No part of this publication may be reproduced, stored in a retrieval system, or transmitted in any form or by any means, electronic, mechanical, photo-copying, recording or otherwise, without prior consent of the publisher. (NOTE: But, if you talk to them in LOVEY DOVEY-ese, betcha you can make them amenable!) 2002 2003 2004 2005 2006/ 10 9 8 7 6 5 4 3 2 1 Printed in China Library of Congress Catalogue Control Number: 2002110264 ... ISBN: 0-7893-0852-5

And a very-lovey-dovey thank you to Taylor Deupree for laying out the book all purty and coloring it in all NICE!

INTRODUCTION

If you're like me, you grew up thinking the French were zee most romantic people. If so, you can imagine my shock when a French beau started calling me un-sexy things like "my flea" and "my little cabbage." In a word: HUH? Then I started thinking about English Lovey Dovey-isms like "honey bunny" and "shnooglywooglyface." (Note: Er....um...is THAT one just MINE?) ♡ Anyway, I got curious- and asked friends for their LOVEY DOVEY-isms ...and got some **doozies**. This book is the sum total of these **wacky international sweet nothings** for you to use and share with your special little cabbage, brought to you with lots of LOVEY DOVEY stuff and wishes....

Love, Karen (Flea) Salmansohn

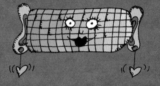

vegetable

"mon pe-tee shoe"

mon petit chou

[MY LITTLE CABBAGE]

FRANCE

"mee-ya mor-kov-ka"

МОЙ МОРКÓВКА

[MY LITTLE CARROT]

RUSSIA

animal

"moya Shop-she-uh"

moja żabcia

[MY LITTLE FROG]

POLAND

" "lit-tel spring-buck"

little springbok

[LITTLE SPRINGBUCK]

SOUTH AFRICA

"esh-kee-pez"

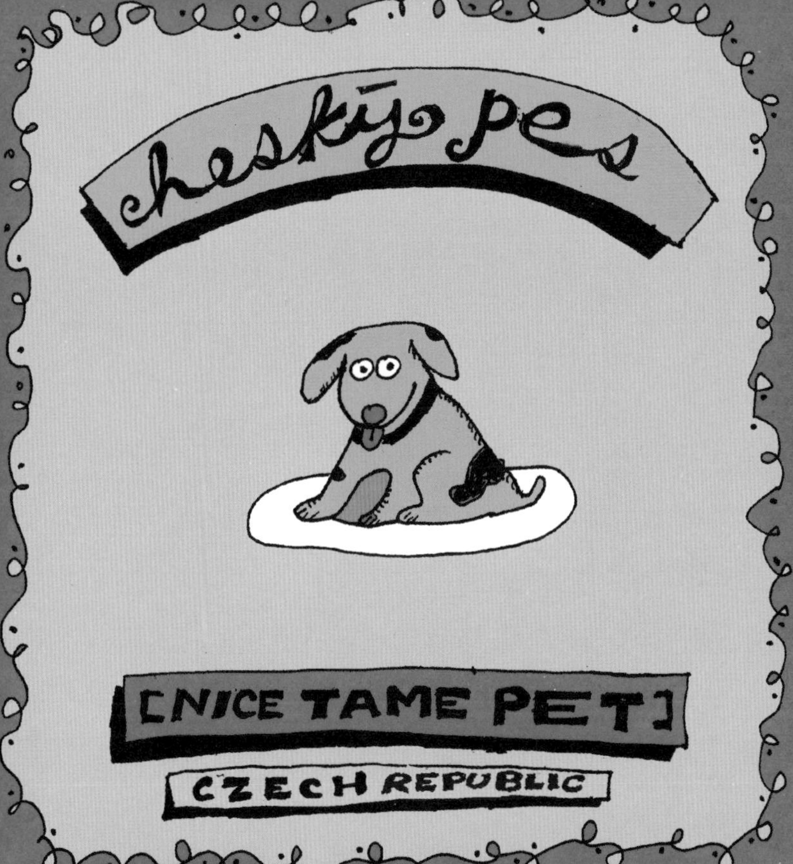

cheskȳ pes
[NICE TAME PET]
CZECH REPUBLIC

"zow-brrr-mouz"

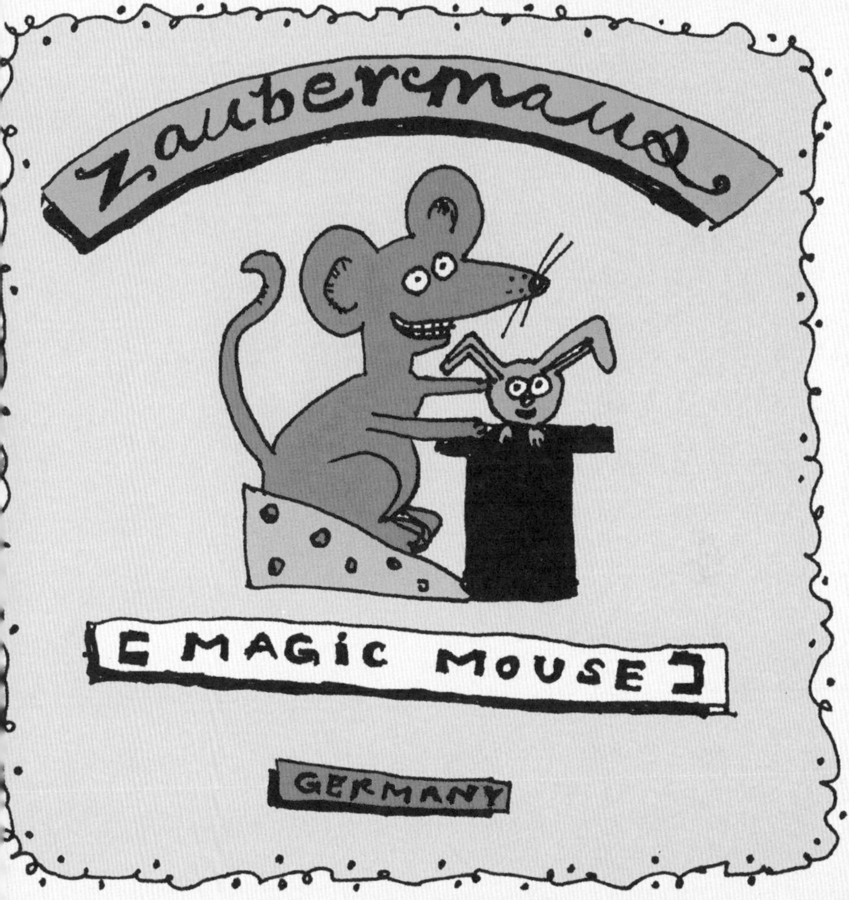
Zaubermaus
[MAGIC MOUSE]
GERMANY

animalfoodhybrid

"shoo-ker-shneck-ke"

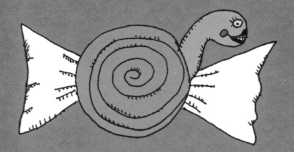

Zuckerschnecke

[SUGAR SNAIL]

GERMANY

"hun-knee bun-knee"

honey bunny

[sweet rabbit]

UNITED STATES of AMERICA

highcaloriccontent

"mmmm"

cupcake

[SMALL CAKE FORMATION]

UNITED STATES of AMERICA

"may-oo doo-see-nyooo-gee co-koo"

"tur-ow-sheen-you gee ah-soo-car"

torrãozinho de açúcar

[MY LITTLE SUGAR CUBE]

PORTUGAL

entomological

"mah-pooos"

ma puce

[MY FLEA]

FRANCE

gardenvariety

"mee-ya mah-kov-ka"

МОЙ МАКОВКА

[MY POPPY SEED]

RUSSIA

* Note: Actual size

"wa-tah-she ro chah-nah"

complimentorinsult

"¡mee-gore-dee-tah!"

mi gordita

[MY FATTY]

EL SALVADOR

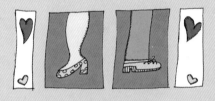

mr/mrsrobinson

"¡ma-ma See-tah!"

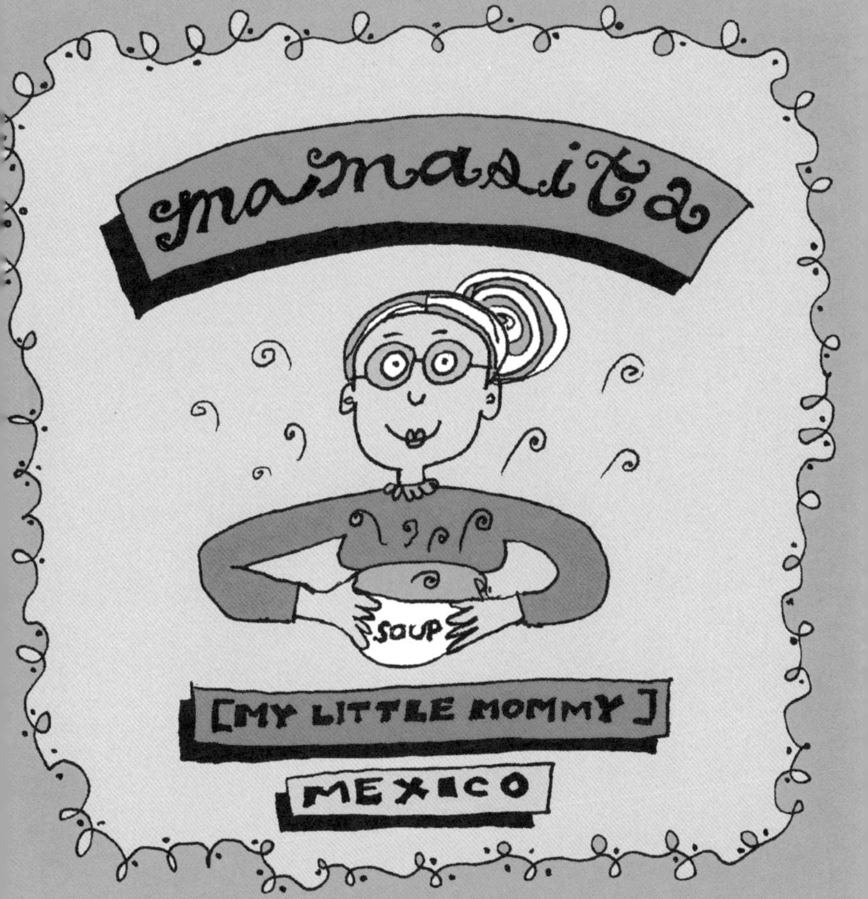
mamasita
SOUP
[MY LITTLE MOMMY]
MEXICO

"yal-dah ki-tan-ah shel-lee"

יַלְדָּה קְטַנָּה שֶׁלִּי

[MY LITTLE GIRL]

ISRAEL

huh?

"Schnooogly-woooogly-faSe"

shnooglywooglyface

[SHNOOGLYWOOGLYFACE]

UNITED STATES of KAREN

"nee-ooo-nya"

"foh-feen-yoo"

fofinho

[LITTLE FLUFFY THING]

PORTUGAL

do-it-yourself-
lovey-dovey-guide

♡ PREFIX ✝	❀ NOUN ✝	♡ SUFFIX
watashi no my / Japanese	**armadillo**	**cia / ek** F/M little / Polish
shooker sugar / German	**sledgehammer**	**inyo / inya** m/f little / Portuguese
moya MY / Polish	**tapioca**	**ita / ito** f/m little / Spanish
mee refrito/a M/F my refried / Spanish	**kneecap**	**gee asookar** of sugar / Portuguese
meeya my / Russian	**mosquito bite**	**ka** little / Russian
zowbrrr magic / German	**pookie**	**shelee** of mine / Hebrew
moh petee / ma peteet M/F mylittle / French	**gigabyte**	**pie** "sweet thang" / English
LINDA / LINDO F/M beautiful / Portuguese	**kidney stone**	**picante** spicy / Spanish

the authorized bio of... ♡
♡ **KAREN SALMANSOHN** ♡

Karen's first **lovey-dovey-name** was **KARONESS** - or at least that's how it sounded when she was 8. She was really being called "Karen S." because there were **3 Karens** in her school class. Karen always liked being **KARONESS**. It made her feel **shnazzy**. Sadly, at age 12, she was returned to mere Karen status when the other Karens switched schools. Later lovey-dovey-esque names became "**Special K**" and "**Ma. puce**." Oh... she's also a **best selling** author whose books include **HOW TO BE HAPPY, DAMMIT** and **THE CLITOURIST: A GUIDE TO ONE OF THE HOTTEST SPOTS ON EARTH**. ❀ ❀ ❀ ❀